TALKING TO STRANGERS

How to master the art of talking to strangers,
overcome fear of rejection, build relationships,
and create a killer first impression

Malcolm Pearce

Malcolm Pearce

COPYRIGHT © 2022 Malcolm Pearce

All rights reserved.

TABLE OF CONTENTS

INTRODUCTION 4
FEAR OF REJECTION 8
   How To Deal with Rejection...8
      How Rejection Fear Limits Your Life 8
      Fearful Behavior's Consequences................................13
      How To Get Rid Of Your Fear Of Rejection 15
      Final thought 17
TALKING TO STRANGERS: THE BUILDING BLOCK
....18
      The opener 18
      Fake time constraint..18
      Opinion Opener..19
      Transitioning...20
      The uneasy part 21
      Connecting and deepening 22
      Deep & wide Conversational rapport 23
      Maintaining contact..24
THE BEST PEOPLE FOR YOU: HOW TO TURN STRANGERS INTO FRIENDS 26
STARTING A CONVERSATION THE RIGHT WAY .34

Getting Started *34*
Conversation Killers *35*
Keep It Positive *37*
Start Simple *38*
Ask for Help *39*
Conversation Starters *39*
Body Language *41*
Listen and show interest *42*
Find A Balance *42*

BODY LANGUAGE TECHNIQUES: HOW TO USE BODY LANGUAGE TO YOUR ADVANTAGE WHEN MEETING STRANGERS..44

HOW TO JOIN A GROUP DISCUSSION (WITHOUT BEING AWKWARD)...50

Talking To Strangers

INTRODUCTION

It is often said that people's greatest fear is speaking in front of an audience. What is less well known is that the second most common fear is talking to strangers. You only have to walk through a bustling city during the day to appreciate it. A dynamic metropolis where people go about their day with little awareness or a clear interest in the people they meet. It's not surprising, however, because from an early age we are culturally inclined to believe statements such as "silence is golden", "expect a good introduction" or "don't talk to strangers".

Perhaps these well-meaning commands had a place and a function in our youth, but in adulthood, they mostly got in the way of how we dealt with others...

In the field of social psychology, there is a specific type of experiment called the breakthrough experiment which has become popular through the work of sociologist Harold Garfinkel.

A breakthrough experience is when you behave in a way that breaks down the "normal social structure". At least what we are conditioned to believe is socially "normal". An example might be going to a vendor with an item of clothing and negotiating a better price, or going to MacDonald's and asking for a sirloin steak, medium rare, with a side of vegetables. Both of these examples go against what is considered the "social norm" in these situations.

The weird thing about breaking up experiences is that it's an incredibly scary experience when you first do it. The reality is that you are completely safe, but you are reacting as if something terrible could happen. But when you do several in a row, something strange happens...You reach a point where this fear suddenly melts.

It's like slowly letting go of the layers of fear and suddenly realizing they never really existed. It is a strange but extremely liberating experience that I would recommend to everyone. When it comes to talking to strangers, many people have hurt themselves to the point where it's like breaking a social norm, thinking it's a horrible experience for the first time.

But if you, do it multiple times, like the breakthrough experiences, you'll have this weird experience of the layer of fear separating and you'll suddenly be hit with the realization that fear never existed. So, my advice is to talk to as many strangers as possible during the day. It doesn't have to go anywhere, just see how far you can push it each time, then get out. You get scared the first few times and every once in a while, you get weird reactions (which is mostly their fault, not you), but pretty soon you have to do it, that fear goes away and you get more and more positive feedback, which leads to great opportunities.

Of course, it helps if you have some sort of strategy for starting a conversation with a stranger and continuing it in a way that makes it interesting and fun. While every conversation is, of course, different and unpredictable, some guidelines will help you tremendously.

In this book, we will go over several sections and sub-topics. We will give you tips on how to get started talking to anyone with minimum effort. You will learn how to communicate with strangers, overcome fear and social anxiety, and become a better version of yourself. If all you want to learn today is how to talk to strangers and create a relationship with them without feeling awkward, this is the only book you need to read today. You won't be able to "talk to strangers" unless you finish all of the parts. Following them all and reviewing them frequently help you keep on track and ensure that you are on the right course.

Talking To Strangers

FEAR OF REJECTION
How To Deal with Rejection

The sting of rejection is named after how it feels when you reach out to pluck a promising "flower" (such as a new love interest, career chance, or friendship) only to be met with an unexpected and upsetting brush-off that feels like an attack. It's enough to make you want to avoid putting yourself out there in the future. You will, however, or you will never find the people or chances who are interested in everything you have to offer.

So, how can you deal with rejection and overcome your fear of being rejected again? The fear of rejection is discussed in this section, as well as how rejection sensitivity can affect your life and conduct. It also goes through some of the techniques you can utilize to get over your fear.

How Rejection Fear Limits Your Life

Although not everyone is afraid of rejection, it has a significant impact on one's capacity to achieve in a variety of personal and professional settings.

Job Interviews

Physical symptoms associated with rejection fear can be misinterpreted as a lack of confidence. Many roles require confidence and an aura of authority, and those who lack these qualities come out as weak and insecure. If you are afraid of rejection, you may find it difficult to negotiate work-related contracts, resulting in the loss of valuable compensation and benefits.

Business Dealings

The need to impress does not go away once you get the job in many cases. Many careers require entertaining clients, making deals, selling products, and recruiting investors. For people who are afraid of rejection, even simple tasks like answering the phone can be terrible.

Making New Friends

Humans are social beings, and we are expected to observe basic social etiquette when we are out in public. If you're afraid of rejection, you could find it difficult to talk to strangers or even friends of friends. Your tendency to isolate yourself may hinder you from forming long-term relationships.

Dating

First dates can be intimidating, but those who are afraid of rejection may feel much more so. Rather than concentrating on getting to know the other person and determining whether or not you want to go on another date, you may spend all of your time pondering whether or not that person is interested in you. Common symptoms include difficulty speaking, constant anxiety about your looks, inability to eat, and a tense mood.

Marriage

Marriage is a never-ending process of compromises and negotiations. Two people can't agree on everything, no matter how compatible they are. Those who are afraid of rejection have a hard time expressing themselves and standing up for themselves.

As your fear of rejection grows into a fear of being abandoned, you may develop sentiments of jealousy or distrust in your relationship. This can manifest itself in harmful activities such as checking your partner's phone messages or social media accounts.

Relationships between peers

People often act in ways that assist them to fit in with the group because they have a basic human need to belong. While looking, speaking, and acting as a group member isn't always detrimental, peer pressure can occasionally be excessive. It may lead you to do things you don't want to do to stay in the group.

The fear of rejection can have an impact on many aspects of your life, including your career success and relationships with friends and romantic partners.

Typical conduct

When you have a fear of rejection, you may engage in a variety of actions aimed at either masking or compensating for your anxiety. These may include the following:

Lack of Authenticity

Many people who are afraid of rejection have a regimented, scripted lifestyle. You may hide behind a mask because you are afraid of being rejected if you reveal your genuine self to the world. This might make you appear false and inauthentic to others, and it can lead to a rigid refusal to accept life's problems.

People-Pleasing

Although it is natural to desire to look after individuals we care about, folks who are afraid of rejection frequently go too far. Even if saying yes creates enormous hassles or troubles in your personal life, you may find it impossible to say no. You may take on too much if you are a people-pleaser, increasing your risk of burnout. People-pleasing can often cross the line into enabling others' harmful behavior.

Passivity

People who are afraid of rejection will go to great lengths to avoid conflicts. You may be unwilling to ask for what you want or even to speak up for what you require. One typical tendency is to try to ignore or shut down your own needs.

You may be preventing yourself from attaining your greatest potential because you are afraid of rejection. Putting yourself out there is scary for everyone, but if you're afraid of being rejected, you might become immobilized. Even if you are unhappy with your existing situation, clinging to the status quo feels safe.

Passive-Aggressiveness

Many people who are afraid of rejection wind up behaving in passive-aggressive ways because they are uncomfortable showing off their genuine selves yet can't completely shut out their wants. You may procrastinate, "forget" to keep promises, whine, and work inefficiently on initiatives.

You might engage in behaviors like passive-aggressiveness, apathy, and people-pleasing because you're afraid of rejection. It can also sabotage your authenticity and make it tough to be yourself in front of others, particularly strangers.

Fearful Behavior's Consequences

Fear of rejection causes insecure, ineffective, and overwhelmed behaviors.

You may sweat, fidget, avoid eye contact, and lose your ability to speak properly. While people react to these behaviors in a variety of ways, the following are some of the reactions you might see.

Rejection

Surprisingly, the dread of rejection frequently becomes self-fulfilling. Confidence boosts beauty, as is generally established in popular psychology. In general, we are more likely to be rejected if we have a lack self-confidence as a result of our fear of rejection. It is widely acknowledged that our level of confidence is nearly as significant as our level of intelligence in determining our income.

Manipulation

Some individuals profit from others' vulnerabilities. Those who are afraid of rejection are more likely to be used for personal benefit by others.

Expert manipulators have a pleasant, sophisticated, and sympathetic demeanor; they know how to make others trust them by pressing the right buttons. They also know how to put someone afraid of rejection on edge, as if the manipulator could abandon them at any moment. After getting what they want from the other person, the manipulator almost always leaves.

Frustration

The vast majority of individuals are decent, truthful, and open. They will try to assist rather than manipulate someone afraid of rejection. Look for evidence that your friends and family are attempting to motivate you to be more forceful by urging you to be more open with them or investigating your genuine feelings.

People who are afraid of rejection, on the other hand, frequently regard these efforts as emotionally damaging. Friends and family typically tread carefully around you, afraid of exacerbating your anxieties. They may become irritated and upset over time, questioning you about your behavior or moving away from you.

How To Get Rid Of Your Fear Of Rejection

If you're afraid of rejection, there are steps you can do to improve your coping skills and prevent your life from being badly impacted by this anxiety. For learning how to overcome a fear of rejection, you may find the following ideas useful:

Enhance your ability to self-regulate

The ability to recognize and manage one's emotions and behaviors is referred to as self-regulation. It's also helpful for conquering rejection fears. You can actively take measures to reframe your thinking in a way that is more hopeful and encouraging by being able to recognize negative thoughts that contribute to feelings of fear.

Confront your fears

Avoidance coping entails avoiding items that cause negative feelings. The problem with this strategy is that it leads to more worry. Instead of helping you overcome your fear of rejection, it makes you even more afraid and vulnerable to it.

Rather than avoiding situations where you might be rejected, concentrate on putting yourself out there and confronting your anxiety. You'll notice that the repercussions are less anxiety-provoking than you expected as you gain more practice facing your fear. You'll have more faith in your ability to succeed as well.

Cultivate Resilience

Being resilient is being able to bounce back from a setback with newfound vigor and confidence. Building confidence in one's talents, having a strong social support system, and nurturing and caring for oneself are all strategies that can help promote a greater sense of resilience. Having objectives and taking measures to enhance your talents can help you believe in your capacity to bounce back after being rejected.

Final thought

Taking actions to overcome your fear of rejection can help you reduce the negative consequences of rejection. Learning to control your emotions, confronting your anxieties, and establishing a strong sense of resilience can all help you cope with rejection fear.

TALKING TO STRANGERS: The Building Block

The opener

The purpose of the opener is of course to initiate the conversation. When talking to a stranger, how you open the conversation can make a huge difference in the quality of the conversation. Here are some quick opening tips:

Fake time constraint

One of the biggest worries people have when coming into contact with a stranger is that they're stuck with a crazy person who doesn't offer much value and is wasting their precious time. It sounds harsh, but it's true. An effective way to prevent yourself from falling into this category is to use fake time pressure. It may not be completely honest, but it will help the conversation immensely. Fake time pressure is when you say something that suggests you can't stay too long. For example, it could be:

"Excuse me, I'm going to a meeting, but I was wondering if you could give me your opinion on something earlier, I'm leaving".

False time constraints work effectively because they let the person know that you aren't some weirdos with nowhere to go and that you won't be taking up too much of their valuable time.

Opinion Opener

With the opinion opener, you start a conversation with a cautious person to ask their opinion on something. Opinion openers work well since there aren't many people who wouldn't be willing to help you out by providing their thoughts on a topic. When you approach strangers, you'll discover that most people are delighted to assist you, and it's a fantastic way to get the conversation started.

Here are some examples of opinion leaders. These will work even if they don't apply to you, but of course work much better if you use such as:

"Sorry, do you know a good restaurant nearby; I'm going out to dinner with a friend this weekend and it would be nice to have a recommendation?'

"Sorry, my girlfriend's birthday is the new week... I don't know what to get her, any idea?"

(In a bookstore) "I'm thinking of reading some new writers, can you recommend one?"

"It may sound strange, but I'm looking for an outside opinion here. I'm having a themed birthday party and I'm a little obsessed with ideas. What do you think?"

These are just a few examples to get you started. Think of some personal opening opinions that you can use to start a conversation with a stranger.

Transitioning

So, if you've been hanging out with the opener, it's time to move on to the normal conversation. There are many ways to do this, but one of the easiest is to simply ask them what their plans are. This opens up more opportunities for other conversations. Another good way is to make a statement about what is happening in the area. Here are some additional transition phrases you can use to get started:

"So where are you going today?" (About a band) "So how do you know each other?" "What are you doing for your life?"

"You know you give good advice; you have to start doing it to live! "So, what do you like to do when you're not advising strangers?" "Oh, by the way, my name is (name), what's your name?" "It's just my second time here and it's an interesting place"

The goal of the transition phase is to reach an attachment point. A catch is when you come across something that both of you are interested in. It doesn't have to be one of your core passions, it just has to be something that both interests you and can talk about.

The uneasy part

You occasionally encounter folks who are easy to chat to and with whom you click easily and without much awkwardness. Most of the time, though, there will be a period where the conversation is a little stifled and awkward at the start. This is entirely normal... remember, you've only just met them, and chances are they're uncomfortable talking to strangers as well, so just relax and ride it out. Continue gently probing with questions and making comments and statements about things, and the uneasiness will ultimately fade away. People frequently want to quit at this time because they think things aren't going well, but if you stick with it, you'll get beyond this stage rather quickly.

Connecting and deepening

So, you started by asking for an opinion, then transitioned into a discussion, and then got over the 'awkward bit.' It's now time to make contact with the individual. There are a couple of ways to do this:

Keyword Latching

Have you been paying attention to what they've been saying to you? Or have you been too preoccupied with figuring out what to say next? Again, don't worry...it'll get better with experience, and you'll soon be able to focus your attention more on the outside and begin to do something called 'keyword latching.'

Latching is when you listen to what someone is saying and then 'latch on to anything important they've stated. They might state, for example, that they enjoy traveling. You could say something along these lines to capitalize on the traveling aspect:

"Oh, that's fascinating. I enjoy going on vacations... Last year, I visited Paris, which is an incredible city... what is the finest destination you've visited?"

When using keyword latching, the challenge is to respond with anything that allows them to latch onto or leads to another question.

Deep & wide Conversational rapport

Deep conversational rapport occurs when you begin a conversation with someone about a topic that they are interested in and then delve deeply into that issue, covering numerous points of view and facets of it... I'm sure you've had the experience of meeting someone with whom you share a passion or an interest, and then spending a significant amount of time chatting to them about it... When this happens, you feel deeply at ease with each other, as if you understand one other on a far deeper level than if you had merely exchanged small conversations.

Wide conversational rapport, on the other hand, is when you discuss a wide range of issues that both of you are interested in. In general, the larger the spectrum of topics you discuss with each other that you both enjoy, the better the sense of mutual rapport and ease you will feel...

You will both begin to have a strong sense of connection that is both natural and honest if you combine this with deep conversational rapport by getting fairly deep into each of the topics.

When you're conversing with someone you've just met, there's a strong possibility you're both on your way somewhere and won't have much time to have a long and significant conversation. Developing a strong and broad verbal connection with someone might develop quickly, but it usually takes a few meetings. So, during the first connection, your goal is to build as much conversational rapport as possible to earn the right to continue in touch. (Of course, if you want to)

Maintaining contact

So, you've begun the conversation, transitioned, handled the awkwardness, and managed to chat about some issues that both of you are interested in. Hopefully, you'll have enough reasons to stay in touch at this point. If you have, the next step is the simplest of them all. If you haven't, hey, nothing ventured, nothing gained; it's all part of the learning process.

In the end, it's only a matter of making the request. Their contact information could be in their phone book, email, or even on Facebook. While complimenting an aspect of their personality can be helpful, the most important thing is to make it clear that it's a matter of fact. As an example: "Hey, you have a nice sense of humor, it'd be great to keep in touch are you on Facebook/email??"

Talking To Strangers

"It's funny, I only stopped to get your take on something, but we've had a lot of fun talking about it... It would be great to get together again, but till then, how can we stay in touch?"

It's not nearly as bad as people make it out to be when it comes to getting someone's personal information. As long as you don't make a fuss about it, they won't either.

Malcolm Pearce

THE BEST PEOPLE FOR YOU: How to Turn Strangers into Friends

"Fear makes strangers of people who would be friends." ~Shirley MacLaine

I used to think of the world as a place where very few doors opened for me until a year ago. I initially assumed it was due to my strong introversion. However, as time passed, I began to have difficulty making acquaintances.

I didn't have many, and opportunities only came up once or twice a year. That's when I recognized my issues were caused by my passivity and fear of actually stepping out and chatting to people. My close pals continually encouraged me to join a club or attend parties. People used to tell me where I could meet people. However, they never showed me how to initiate a discussion.

Furthermore, I have never enjoyed attending large social gatherings. I'm an introvert who gets overwhelmed when there are a lot of people around. I enjoy one-on-one conversations. So, I decided to go my own way. I became weary of standing on the sidelines and started talking to people on my college campus and in the city. It was terrifying for me as a typically hesitant person, but I resolved to face my fears. Great things come to those who are willing to put themselves out there and risk rejection.

I made some amazing friends after two months of doing this just by starting conversations. It's a liberating mindset to be able to strike up a conversation with anyone. I always have the option of talking to anyone I want.

I inquired as to what coffee shop beverage they had purchased. I inquired about her customized bicycle. I asked for people's thoughts on issues that affected me. Some folks were willing to talk to me. Some folks remained inactive. When I put the spotlight on them, some of them continued to talk about themselves. Others merely replied to my question and then walked away. All of these interactions taught me how to communicate with others. I learned, for example, that tone and body language are more essential than stating the correct thing.

People are generally friendly and happy to talk to you, based on my experiences. I have met more individuals than I ever thought simply by being open with them.

That's when I realized it was up to me to take charge and open my doors rather than lamenting about how none were opening for me. It was up to me to interact with individuals and generate my abilities.

Aside from feeling more connected, I'm happy knowing that I can communicate with whomever I want. Networking with others led to more opportunities. For example, because I reached out and asked, I was able to study photography with a new acquaintance.

Here are 11 strategies for turning strangers into friends that I learned:

Say "Hi," the magic word

It may seem obvious, yet it is the first major roadblock. To initiate a discussion, you must be willing to put yourself out there.

After you break the ice, I've discovered that people are more welcoming. It's not something everyone wants to do because approaching someone you've never met and striking up a conversation takes courage. However, more people are hospitable than we may assume. Remember that someone else will be when you meet someone who isn't.

Remove yourself from the result

You won't be disappointed or offended if someone doesn't respond to you if you don't anticipate anything.

There is a distinction between what is expected and what occurs. How many times have you fretted about the worst-case scenario just to discover that it turned out to be a lot better than you expected?

If I don't expect anything to happen as a result of whatever I'm doing, I can be present at the moment and adjust accordingly.

Accept criticism

It's not about you if they reject you. Don't take it personally; it's about where they're at mentally. If they didn't take advantage of the opportunity to connect with you, they missed out on something wonderful.

Don't give a damn what other people think

This is your life, and you have the freedom to speak with anyone you want. Not everyone is as forthcoming. Allow them to be who they are and think what they think without putting your courage in jeopardy.

If you feel the fear, do it anyway

Repetition is one of the most effective techniques to overcome fear. Push past your fear and it will begin to feel more normal.

The fear may never go away completely, but if you keep fighting through it, the momentum you build will be stronger than the dread itself. When I'm afraid of approaching someone, for example, I recall a relaxing or humorous experience. The fear didn't seem as frightening after that.

Practice

Don't be concerned if you appear awkward or pushy at first. If your objectives are genuine, you will notice them more and more with each attempt.

It's the same with any other skill: practice makes perfect. A handful of my initial encounters with strangers were frightening and unpleasant, but they didn't injure me. It taught me what I needed to improve on.

Make it all about them

Discuss their passions, beliefs, and views. Then react to what they've said.

Showing an interest in someone's life is the best approach to keep them engaged in a conversation. Everyone enjoys discussing themselves. Keep asking questions to learn more about a subject, even if you don't know much about it.

Make them laugh out loud

Laughter adds to the enjoyment of the talk. People appreciate conversing with someone who can make them laugh. So, get out of your thoughts and don't take yourself too seriously—just enjoy yourself!

Try to figure out what their true passion is

If their eyes light up when they talk about something, follow up with extra inquiries.

If you come across a keyword that helps you figure out what they're interested in, bring it up. If I asked, "How's the weather?" for example. "It's wonderful that it's foggy since," they say. It is preferable to run in it." Then you may start talking about running.

Go out and smile!

A positive first impression is made through smiling. Practice in front of the mirror. Then give the world a grin.

When I smiled first, I noticed that people become calmer. They smiled back and opened up to deeper talk when I kept smiling throughout the session.

Imagine that the other person is already your friend

This way, instead of appearing uneasy, you'll treat them as such—and being at ease around someone is the ideal approach to begin a new friendship.

Take a chance today and strike up a conversation with someone new. When you are friendly to someone, they will usually return the favor.

STARTING A CONVERSATION THE RIGHT WAY

Some people seem to have a natural talent for making small talk, while others struggle. Knowing how to start a conversation is a vital social skill. Knowing how to start a conversation can help you feel more comfortable and confident in a wide range of social circumstances, whether you're trying to impress a potential customer, strike up a conversation with a love interest, or simply chat with a new friend.

Getting Started

Going to a party or a work function can be terrifying if being in a room full of strangers is your worst nightmare. If you're introverted, or socially anxious, these kinds of social encounters might be particularly challenging.

Preparing ahead of time is one approach to reducing stress. Rehearse with a friend or reread what you want to say in your head. Being well-prepared is the first step toward becoming a fantastic conversationalist.

If you're hesitant to initiate a conversation, try one of these three basic tactics first:

Keep a good attitude: Stop worrying about making a mistake and trust yourself. Worrying too much about what you'll say next can lead to you losing track of what's going on in the conversation. Rather, concentrate on the other person and what they're saying.

Take a deep breath: You're less likely to feel relaxed if you're tight and nervous. Maintain a calm demeanor and allow the talk to flow freely.

Let me start by saying hello: One of the simplest methods to get started is to simply introduce yourself and then allow the other person to do the same. After this initial icebreaker, ask a basic question or make a simple observation to spark additional conversation.

Conversation Killers

While it should go without saying, there are a few things you should avoid unless you are familiar with the person you are chatting with.

While your uncle may start conversations with political commentary, gossip, complaints, and offensive jokes at family gatherings, this is not an example you should try to follow in your daily life. When starting talks, stay away from anything offensive, provocative, or uncomfortable. There is a time and place for expressing your views or even trying to persuade others, but make sure that such issues are acceptable before getting into a heated discussion.

According to some studies, the greatest way to start a discussion is to make harmless remarks. Participants were asked to judge the success of a variety of starting lines that could come from a potential love partner, including sarcastic "pick-up" lines, open-ended, harmless queries, and a direct approach, in one study.

The pick-up line method was disliked by a large number of respondents, but opinions on the other two opening styles were divided. Men preferred the more direct approach ("I'd like to buy you a drink!") whereas women preferred benign queries ("What's your favorite team?").

When it comes to striking up a conversation with a stranger, the study's authors say that it's preferable to go for the safe option. This form of conversation starter is less intimidating, yet it still prompts the other person to respond in some way.

Keep It Positive

Start on a positive note. Don't start a rant or make a snarky remark. You can always find something pleasant to say, regardless of the scenario. Make a remark about the weather, the food, the people in attendance, or the event itself. It's an excellent technique to start a discussion by saying something simple like "I'm having a good time" and hoping your conversation partner is having a good time as well. Try to see the bright side of the circumstance, even if it isn't ideal.

Lead With Remarks:

"Wasn't that a fantastic demonstration?"

"Whoever put this event together did an outstanding job!"

"You gave a wonderful presentation. I feel as if I've gained a great deal of knowledge!"

"Today is extremely cold, but the weather forecast predicts a pleasant and sunny day tomorrow."

A favorable comment is more likely to be received favorably than a negative comment. It demonstrates that you are a friendly individual who is aware of current events. It also helps to put folks at ease if you keep a happy attitude. People will be more inclined to continue a conversation with you as a result.

Start Simple

A big, philosophical, earth-shattering insight isn't required to start every great conversation. Simple icebreaker remarks or inquiries are an excellent place to start.

Although remarking on the weather, the accommodation, or the cuisine may seem cliched, there is a reason why this type of icebreaker is so effective. It's a basic, straightforward technique to start a discussion by providing some common ground between two strangers. Talking about trivial matters can lead to deeper discussions about personal preferences, backgrounds, hobbies, and other issues that might help people form social relationships.

What Research Says

Researchers in one study published in the journal Psychological Science conducted naturalistic observations on individuals over several days to record both casual chats and serious conversations.

They discovered that persons who engaged in more in-depth, personal talks were also happier. This could indicate that happy people are more likely to engage in meaningful interactions with others, but it could also indicate that such serious conversations contribute to increased happiness.

In their study, researchers found that "the happy life is social rather than isolated, and conversationally profound rather than shallow."

Small talk isn't for everyone, but it can be a vital first step toward deeper, more significant talks. While it's common to start a discussion with small talk, research reveals that having more in-depth conversations is associated with better happiness and well-being. Learning how to initiate a conversation will assist you in making more meaningful social connections.

Ask for Help

A good technique to start a conversation is to ask a question. This not only provides you a purpose to interact with the other person, but it also allows them to assist you.

Start with something easy that requires little work while using this method. For example, you might inquire about the start time of a workshop or directions to a specific location.

Conversation Starters

"Do you know where I could get a schedule?"

"Did you notice an earring?" I believe I've misplaced one."

"Do you know if refreshments will be offered after the workshop?"

Asking a basic inquiry might lead to more discussion about other issues, which is one of the advantages of this method. Once you've asked your inquiry and the other person has offered to help, you and your conversation partner have formed a kind of reciprocal social contract.

You should now express your gratitude and introduce yourself, as they have given their support. This is an excellent time to learn more about the other person, including who they are, what brought them here, and other pertinent questions given the environment and situation.

Preparing ahead of time is one strategy to reduce worry. Review what you want to say in your head, and practice with a friend if possible. Being prepared is the first step toward becoming a fantastic conversationalist. If you're concerned about starting a conversation, try one of these three basic techniques first:

Stop worrying about making a mistake and trust in your ability instead: Worrying too much about what you'll say next can cause you to lose track of what's going on in the conversation. Rather, concentrate on the other person and what they are saying.

Take a deep breath: You're less likely to feel at ease if you're tense and nervous. Maintain a calm demeanor and allow the talk to flow naturally.

Introduce yourself: One of the easiest methods to get started is to simply introduce yourself and then allow the other person to do the same. After this initial icebreaker, try asking a basic question or making a simple observation to spark additional conversation.

Body Language

Sometimes what you do not say is as important as what you say. When starting a new conversation, it's important to pay attention to your non-verbal communication.

Body language can be used to express interests and feelings. For example, a friendly facial expression, pleasant demeanor, and good eye contact can show that you're genuinely interested in learning more about someone else. On the other hand, your interviewer may be bored or uninterested.

Encouraging non-verbal cues include:

An open stance, keeping the body open with the arms relaxed, contributes to a feeling of togetherness.

Looking someone in the eyes is what good eye contact entails. Don't die, it can be threatening. Instead, keep it natural, look into the other person's eyes, but look away from time to time. Smiling can help, as long as it looks real and natural. Avoid faking a big smile and try to invest in a relaxed yet uplifting expression.

Listen and show interest

It can be scary talking to someone when you feel like you have something in common. In these situations, the other person talking about their interests, work, or expertise can be a good conversation starter.

Ask a question about what the other person is doing, then focus on listening to what they have to say. People often like to talk about things that are close to their hearts, so showing a genuine interest in the things other people like can be a great spark for good conversation.

Find A Balance

A good conversation does not rely on a single approach. The best conversations are about asking questions, listening to what others have to say, and sharing things about yourself.

A simple conversation can start with:

- Ask for some basic information ("Do you like the presentation?")
- Listen to the reaction ("That was awesome! I feel like I learned a lot!")
- Express your thoughts ("I think so too. I already have ideas on how to incorporate these tips into my work process.")

You can then repeat the process by asking another question, or your interviewer can choose to ask a question about your previous answer.)

You might also think it's good to ask open-ended questions that can't just be answered with "yes" or "no." For example, you might ask "What do you think of the narrator?" instead of "Do you like the narrator?"

Learning to start a conversation is an important skill that can help you socialize in a variety of settings. It can be difficult at first, especially if you suffer from embarrassment or social anxiety, but getting enough exercise is key to becoming more comfortable talking to other people. Try to view each of these interactions as training. The more you talk to others, the stronger your ability to speak.

BODY LANGUAGE TECHNIQUES: How To Use Body Language To Your Advantage When Meeting Strangers

Meeting new people can be a frightening experience for some of us. Others see it as an exciting and educational adventure. You'll encounter new people in your life in either case, and it's in your best interest to make a good first impression.

It's not always simple to make a good first impression, especially if you're in a new place and don't know what to say. To assure a positive response, engage in a pleasant conversation, and eventually leave with an acquaintance, there is some body language "hacks" you can utilize.

When you go to a networking event (or each time you meet new people), try some of these moves:

Take a powerful stance

This exploit occurs even before you enter the room. According to research, "power postures" can fool your brain into feeling more confident, making communication simpler and giving you a more poised appearance. Standing tall and raising your fists in the air, or taking up space by putting your hands on your hips, are examples of this. Do this for 30 seconds to a minute, and you'll feel more confident walking into that room.

Keep your posture "open"

Your body language can reveal a lot about what you're thinking or feeling. People will assume you're not interested in conversing if your body posture is "closed," such as when your arms are folded or your head is down. You'll be perceived as welcoming and friendly if your posture is "open," with your shoulders back and your head up.

Make contact (when appropriate)

When you touch someone, you create an instant connection with them, which is why shaking hands leaves a lasting impression when you first meet them. Give a handshake and, where appropriate, other types of physical contact, such as a touch on the shoulder of your new acquaintance. Just remember to keep things in proportion: Unwelcome contact has more negative than positive influence, especially in male-female interactions.

Take a firm stand

Standing up straight can help you meet new people for a variety of reasons: First, you'll feel and appear more confident, which will provide you an advantage in an interview. Second, your posture will automatically become more "open" and welcoming. Finally, it will allow you to breathe more deeply and healthily during the talk, providing your words more strength and oxygen to your lungs.

Establish eye contact

This isn't merely an old wives' tale or a relic of a bygone era. There are numerous psychological aspects at play when two people make eye contact. Many nonverbal signs are communicated through the eyes, many of which you are probably unaware of. This is one of the reasons that making eye contact with someone instantaneously increases your trust in them, even if only a little.

It also demonstrates that you're paying attention and invested in the discourse. Make early eye contact and keep it whenever possible.

Gesticulation

Making occasional gestures with your arms and hands can help others understand what you're saying. Punching the air can help you highlight a particular point. An upward-turned hand might make a request more welcoming if you wish to ask someone else's opinion.

The real hazard is not the type of gestures you can make, but the frequency with which you make them. You'll come across as a little crazy if you make too many gestures. So, keep your gestures to a minimum.

Do not move

It's not necessary to maintain absolute stillness throughout the interaction; doing so can make you appear robotic. However, you should avoid any fidgeting or motions that disrupt the dialogue. Pacing, tapping your foot, or wringing your hands, for example, can make you appear uneasy and insecure. Instead, attempt to maintain as much control and control over yourself (and your appendages) as possible. This will make you appear more assured.

These body-language tricks won't make up for a boring discussion or a harsh disposition, but they'll get you off to a good start with almost everyone. If you're still unsure about these tricks, practice them with friends or family members, or even in front of the mirror, until you feel comfortable with them.

Talking To Strangers

Malcolm Pearce

How To Join A Group Discussion (Without Being Awkward)

The ability to participate transparently in discussions is an important social skill. When you're at a party or hanging out with strangers, you can approach a group or person with the certainty that you feel involved and have the opportunity to make new friends.

When most people think about it, they see themselves at the party and want to join the ranks of people who are already talking. There are more mundane occasions where we may also wish to talk, such as at a new workplace or a hobby club where we want to chat with colleagues or peers.

Before trying to talk to a group of people, try to get a sense of how open or closed they are. Some groups are made up of close friends who discuss topics that are specific to them. Others are happy when a new one joins them. However, if you can't read them properly and accidentally try to join their conversations, that's not the worst thing that can happen.

In group discussions, everyone talks to everyone, so as you participate in the discussion, continue to encourage this dynamic. Don't sneak into a group, start chatting with one person, and ignore the others.

Sit With The Group, Listen To The Conversation And Participate As Needed

Sometimes that means physically joining a group of people to chat or sit down with them. You may be able to do this quietly, or it may be appropriate to greet or greet everyone. If you know someone in the group, you can greet them quietly and then sit next to them. In other situations, like sitting in a break room at work, you can't join the group, but you're close and you hear what they're talking about. Either way, whenever you see an opportunity to add something relevant, jump into your post and then join the conversation. Be sure to take a short break before you begin. They don't want to be ashamed of cutting anyone off.

Introduce yourself to everyone

At parties, mixes, or networking events, it's often a good idea to just walk into a group and quickly introduce yourself if they seem friendly and open. "Hey, how are you? I'm

Heather" is all you need. However, participating in a conversation can change the course by focusing on you or letting everyone ask introductory questions. Sometimes you want to introduce yourself, but don't interrupt too much. You can quickly say your name, then say something like, "Anyway, what were you talking about earlier?"

Start Conversations With The Group Like You Would With A Single Individual And See How It Goes

It can work with unknown groups at events such as parties. Assuming the group is open to contact, you can use the chat starters described in this article. Instead of talking to just one person, just talk about the group as a whole. You need to adjust them and try to get an idea of what kind of opening line they would be receptive to. Some examples:

In your usual situation, ask, "How did you (the party host) find out?"

Situation Response: "This apartment is so beautifully decorated"

Ask them a question about themselves: "Has anyone been to any good gigs here lately?"

Talking To Strangers

Make a statement about him: "You all seem to have known each other for a long time."

Ask or comment on an outside topic: "Did anyone here play the game last night?"

Make a statement about yourself: (To a group of people you already know a bit about) "The craziest thing that happened to me this weekend..."

"Do you mind if I sit here?"

If you're already friendly enough to hang out and chat with a group, you can sometimes join in their conversations by asking if you can sit down and join them. I think of situations where someone at work is having lunch together and sees a group of coworkers they want to meet, or a student sees a group of acquaintances at a café on campus. When you sit down, they start chatting directly with you or continue what they were talking about, but now you are part of it. It might sound confusing, but the idea is to only do this with people you're already pretty sure you'd want to join.

Talk to someone in the group to get your foot in the door

If you see a larger group of people, the stranger may be someone focused on something else or looking outside, or not interested in the topic everyone is talking about. When you strike up a conversation with this person, you may be able to focus on a larger group and talk to them all. Try this with people who don't seem to deal. If someone is interested and is participating in the conversation, don't try to suck them off.

A similar strategy is to wait until a group member is alone (e.g., if they have gone to a party to drink). You can talk to them when they are alone and join other friends later.

Join The Conversation With An Activity

Parties often feature activities such as beer pong, video games, card games, or board games. Sometimes you can start a conversation by participating in the activity quietly, for example, B. Sit down at a table when a game of flip cup is announced. Then, right from the start, you will naturally have the opportunity to chat with other players. In the pub, you can ask the group if they want to play double pool or table football.

If The Group Is Not Receptive To You

Sometimes people fear that if a group rejects them, they will be rejected in a very harsh and humiliating way. Usually, that doesn't happen, especially if you approach them nicely and don't hit them aggressively or anything. It usually happens that they respond to you symbolically and without commitment, then continue the conversation between themselves and leave you aside. Now, most people are getting the message across and moving forward calmly. It's a little clumsy when it happens, but it's not fucking surgery. To an outsider, it doesn't look like much happened either.

Of course, this shouldn't be confused with a group that lets you join, but they just don't bother to include you in the discussion because they expect you to take the initiative to participate. Then you become a quiet person on the edge and when you feel marginalized and rejected there is more between your ears. They want to involve you in the conversation, you just have to make an effort.